The MOM Dictionary

drawings by:

Valerie McKeown

ADULTS: Group of people Mom longs to communicate with after several hours of talking in small words about topics like "who touched who first."

3

AIRPLANE: What Mom impersonates to get a 1-year-old to eat strained beets.

ALIEN: What Mom would suspect had invaded her house if she spotted a child-sized creature cleaning up after itself.

APPLE: Nutritious lunchtime dessert which kids trade for cupcakes.

BABY: 1) Dad, when he gets a cold. 2) Mom's youngest child, even if he's 42.

BATHROOM: A room used by the entire family, believed by all except Mom to be self-cleaning.

BECAUSE: Mom's reason for having kids do things which can't be explained logically.

BED AND BREAKFAST: Two things the kids will never make for themselves.

7

CARPET: Expensive floor covering used to catch spills and clean mud off shoes.

CAR POOL: Complicated system of transportation where Mom always winds up going the furthest with the biggest bunch of kids who have had the most sugar.

CHINA: Legendary nation reportedly populated by children who love leftover vegetables.

COOK: 1) Act of preparing food for consumption. 2) Mom's other name.

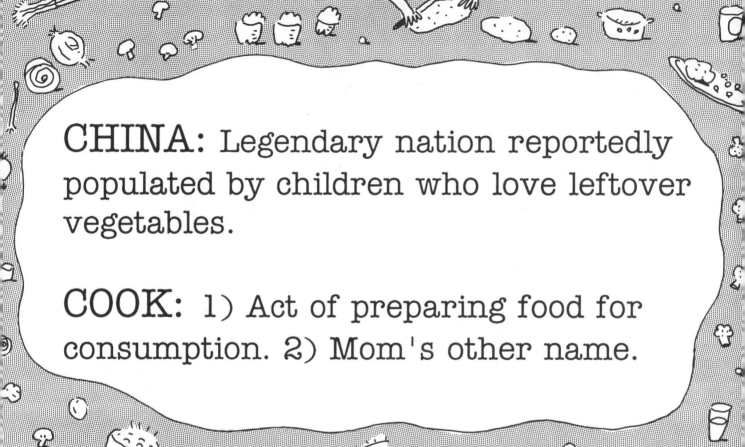

COUCH POTATO: What Mom finds under the sofa cushions after the kids eat dinner.

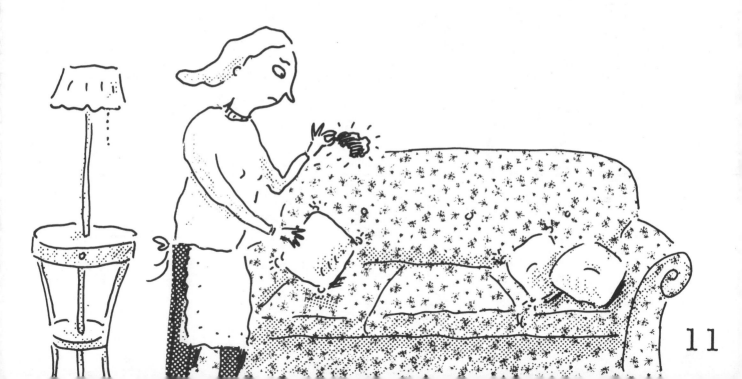

11

DATE: Infrequent outings with Dad where Mom can enjoy worrying about the kids in different settings.

DRINKING GLASS: Any carton or bottle left open in the refrigerator.

DUST: Insideous interloping particles of evil that turn a home into a battle zone.

DUST RAGS: See "Dad's Underwear."

EAR: A place where kids store dirt.

EAT: What kids do between meals, but not at them.

EMPTY NEST: See "Wishful Thinking."

ENERGY: Element of vitality kids always have an oversupply of until asked to do something.

"EXCUSE ME": One of Mom's favorite phrases, reportedly used in past times by children.

EYE: The highly susceptible optic nerve which, according to Mom, can be "put out" by anything from a suction-cup arrow to a carelessly handled butter knife.

FABLE:
A story told
by a teenager
arriving home
after curfew.

FOOD: The response Mom usually
gives in answer to the question
"What's for dinner tonight?" See
"Sarcasm"

19

FROZEN: 1) A type of food. 2) How hell will be when Mom lets her daughter date a guy with a motorcycle.

GARBAGE: A collection of refuse items, the taking out of which Mom assigns to a different family member each week, then winds up doing herself.

GENIUSES: Amazingly, all of Mom's kids.

21

GUM: Adhesive for the hair.

HAMPER: A wicker container with a lid, usually surrounded by, but not containing, dirty clothing.

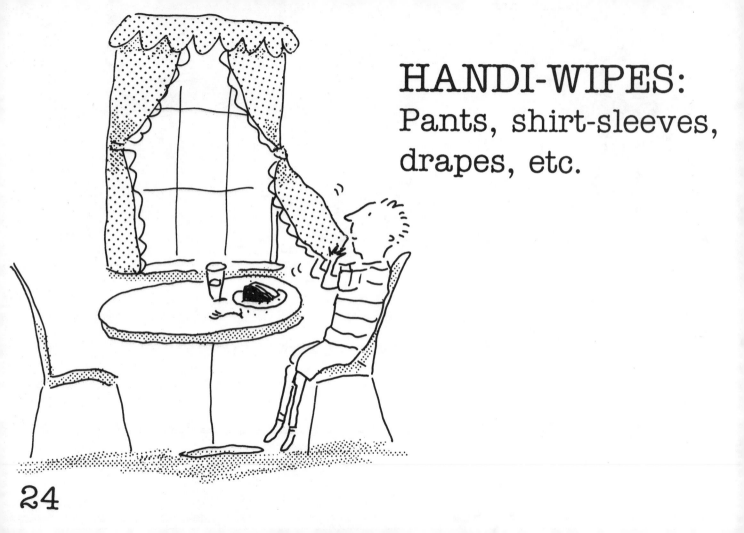

HANDI-WIPES:
Pants, shirt-sleeves, drapes, etc.

24

HANDS: Body appendages which must be scrubbed raw with volcanic soap and sterilized in boiling water immediately prior to consumption of the evening meal.

HINDSIGHT: What Mom experiences from changing too many diapers.

HOMEMADE BREAD: An object of fiction like the Fountain of Youth and the Golden Fleece.

ICE: Cubes of frozen water which would be found in small plastic trays if kids or husbands ever filled the darn things instead of putting them back in the freezer empty.

INSIDE: That place that will suddenly look attractive to kids once Mom has spent half an hour getting them ready to go outside.

"I SAID SO": Reason enough, according to Mom.

JACKPOT: When all the kids stay at friends' homes for the night.

JEANS: Clothing which, according to kids, are appropriate for just about any occasion, including church and funerals.

"JEEEEEEZ!": Slang for "Gee Mom, isn't there anything else you can do to embarrass me in front of my friends?"

31

JOY RIDE: Going somewhere without the kids.

JUNK: Dad's stuff.

KETCHUP: The sea of tomato-based goop kids use to drown the dish that Mom spent hours cooking and years of perfecting to get the seasoning just right.

KISS: Mom medicine.

LAKE: Large body of water into which a kid will jump should his friends do so.

LEMONADE STAND: Complicated business venture where Mom buys powdered mix, sugar, lemons and paper cups, and sets up a table, chairs, pitchers and ice for kids who sit there for three to six minutes and net a profit of 15 cents.

37

LIE: An "exaggeration" Mom uses to transform her child's papier-mache' volcano science project into a Nobel Prize-winning experiment and a full-ride scholarship to Harvard.

LOSERS: See "Kids' Friends"

MAKEUP: Lipstick, eyeliner, blush, etc., which ironically make Mom look better while making her young daughter look "like a tramp."

MAYBE: No.

– Maybe

can I have
a skateboard
like Joe's
for my
birthday?

MILK: A healthful beverage which kids will gladly drink once it's turned into junk food by the addition of sugar and cocoa.

"MOMMMM!": The cry of a child on another floor who wants something.

MUSH: 1) What a kid loves to do with a plateful of food. 2) Main element of Mom's favorite movies.

NAILS: A hard covering on the end of the finger, which Mom can never have a full set of due to pitching for batting practice, opening stubborn modeling clay lids and removing heat ducts to retrieve army men or doll clothing.

OCEAN: What the bathroom floor looks like after bath night for kids, assorted pets, two or three full-sized towels and several dozen toy boats, cars and animals.

OPEN: The position of children's mouths when they eat in front of company.

OVERSTUFFED RECLINER:
Mom's nickname for Dad.

46

PENITENTIARY: Where children who don't eat their vegetables or clean their rooms eventually end up, according to Mom.

I'll eat one more pea... okay Mom?

PETS: Small, furry creatures which follow kids home so Mom will have someone else to clean up after.

PIANO: A large, expensive musical instrument which, after thousands of dollars worth of lessons and constant harping by Mom, kids will refuse to play in front of company.

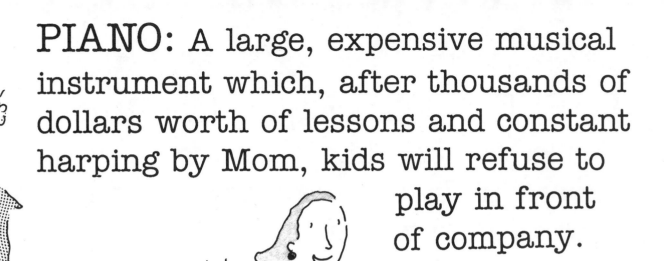

PURSE: A handbag in which Mom carries the checkbook and keys she can never find because they're buried under tissues, gum wrappers, a plastic container full of cereal, toys from a fast-food restaurant, a teddy bear, a football, wallpaper samples, a grocery list and several outdated coupons.

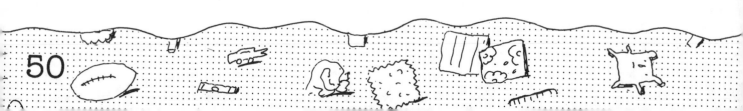

QUIET: A state of household serenity which occurs before the birth of the first child and occurs again after the last child has left for college.

RAINCOAT: Article of clothing Mom bought to keep a child dry and warm, rendered ineffective because it's in the bottom of a locker stuffed in a book bag, or because the child refuses to wear "that geeky thing."

REFRIGERATOR:
Combination art gallery and air-conditioner for the kitchen.

ROOM MOTHER:
A position of great honor and responsibility bestowed on a mom who inadvertently misses a PTA meeting.

SCHOOL PLAY: Sadistic ritual in which adults derive pleasure from watching offspring stumble through coarse reinactments of famous historic events.

SCREAMING: Home P.A. system.

SNOWSUITS: Warm, padded outer garments that, when completely zipped and snapped perform two important functions: Protecting children from the cold and reminding them that they have to go to the bathroom.

SOAP: A cleaning agent Mom puts on the washbasin on the off-chance one of her kids will accidentally grab it while reaching for the towel.

SPIT: All-purpose cleaning fluid especially good on kids' faces.

SPOILED ROTTEN: What the kids become after as little as 15 minutes with Grandma.

SWEATER: Magically charmed article of clothing that can ward away colds, flu and even pneumonia.

SUNDAY BEST: Attractive, expensive children's clothing made of a fabric which attracts melted chocolate and grape juice.

TEACHER CONFERENCE: A meeting between Mom and that person who has yet to understand her child's "special needs."

TERRIBLE TWO'S: Having both kids at home all summer.

"THAT WAY": How kids shouldn't look at moms if they know what's good for them.

TOWELS: See "Floor Coverings"

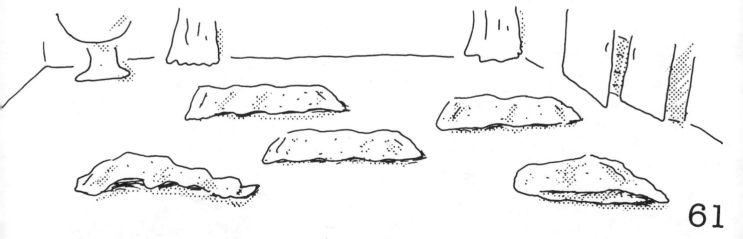

TRAMP: A woman with two kids and no stretch marks.

TROUBLE: Area of nonspecific space a child can always be sure to be in.

UMPTEENTH: Highly conservative estimate of the number of times Mom must instruct her offspring to do something before it actually gets done.

UNDERWEAR: An article of clothing, the cleanliness of which ensures the wearer will never have an accident.

UTOPIA: See "Bubble Bath"

VACATION: Where you take the family to get away from it all, only to find it there, too.

VITAMINS: Tiny facsimiles of cave people Mom forces you to swallow each morning as part of her sinister plot to have you grow up to be "Just like Daddy."

WALLS: Complete set of drawing paper for kids that comes with every room.

WASHING MACHINE: Household appliance used to clean blue jeans, permanent ink markers, loose change, homework, tissues and wads of gum.

67

"WHEN YOUR FATHER GETS HOME": Standard measurement of time between crime and punishment.

XOXOXO: Mom salutation guaranteed to make the already embarrassing note in a kid's lunch box even more mortifying.

XYLOPHONE: Small toy musical instrument often given as gifts to children who show their appreciation by playing the stupid thing constantly, over and over, all day long! See also "Drums"

YARD SALE: Heart-wrenching emotional process wherein Mom plans to sell kids' outdated toys and clothing that she decides at the last minute are treasured mementos she can't bear to part with.

"YIPPEE!": What Mom would jump up and shout if the school year was changed to 12 months. See "Yahoo!"

ZILLION: Amount of times Mom must have gone to the supermarket already this week.

ZUCCHINI: Vegetable which can be baked, boiled, fried or steamed before kids refuse to eat it.

Other books from
SHOEBOX GREETINGS
(A tiny little division of Hallmark)

HEY GUY, ARE YOU: A) Getting Older? B) Getting Better? C) Getting Balder?

FRISKY BUSINESS: All About Being Owned by a Cat.

THE WORLD ACCORDING TO DENISE.

GIRLS JUST WANNA HAVE FACE LIFTS: The Ugly Truth About Getting Older.

DON'T WORRY, BE CRABBY: Maxine's Guide to Life.

EVERYTHING YOU ALWAYS WANTED TO KNOW ABOUT STRESS...but were too nervous, tense, irritable and moody to ask.

40: THE YEAR OF NAPPING DANGEROUSLY.

RAIDERS OF THE LOST BARK: A Collection of Canine Cartoons.

THE DAD DICTIONARY.

WAKE UP AND SMELL THE FORMULA: The A to No ZZZZ's of Having a Baby.

WORKIN' NOON TO FIVE: The Official Workplace Quizbook.

THE OFFICIAL COLLEGE QUIZ BOOK.

WHAT...ME, 30?

STILL MARRIED AFTER ALL THESE YEARS.

YOU EXPECT ME TO SWALLOW THAT?: The Official Hospital Quiz Book.

THE GOOD, THE PLAID, AND THE BOGEY: A Glossary of Golfing Terms.

THE COLLEGE DICTIONARY: A Book You'll Actually Read!

THE FISHING DICTIONARY: Everything You'll Say About the One That Got Away.